The PHOTOGRAPHY Book

Edward Stokes

SCHOLASTIC INC.
New York Toronto London Auckland Sydney

Acknowledgment

Thanks to Olympus, R Gunz and Bob Pattie for help with Olympus cameras and lenses.

Edward Stokes

Previously published in Australia by Ashton Scholastic Pty Limited.

ISBN 0-590-45257-6

12 11 10 9 8 7 6 5 4 3 2 1   2 3 4 5 6 7/9

Printed in the U.S.A.   08

First Scholastic printing, January 1992

CONTENTS

DISCOVERING PHOTOGRAPHY

Photography is fun. It's exciting. And anyone can do it: young kids, older kids—anyone! You don't need a complicated camera to take stunning photos. But you do need some hints, and lots of practice . . .

The art of seeing

Taking photos is a wonderful way of expressing yourself and exploring your world. Wherever you are, fascinating photos are waiting to be taken. But you have to learn to **see** them. 'The art of seeing' is something everyone can develop—and it's your 'seeing eye' which will make great photos.

This book is about discovering how to take photos and about learning how to improve them. It also explains how to use your photos: printing them, presenting them, sharing them with other people.

People are often disappointed with their first photos. Don't despair: learn from your mistakes! Think of your photos as a journey—an exciting, rewarding journey towards better and better photos.

Remember, most famous photographers began just as you are—reading about photography, then practising, practising, practising. Who knows? One day you might even become a working photographer, adventuring around the world with your cameras and film.

5

Photos, photos everywhere

You probably see hundreds of photos every day, from the moment you wake until you collapse into bed:

- on bedroom posters and cereal packets
- in newspapers and magazines
- on billboards
- in books
- on TV.

Try keeping a list of all the photos you see in a single day.

Taking photos means **you** can make **your own** personal record.

DISCOVERING PHOTOGRAPHY

The world according to you!

You could draw all the interesting things you see or you could write about them, but nothing is quite as magical as taking a photo and looking at it later. And not everyone **can** draw. If you're a frustrated artist, why not pick up a camera?

You could photograph:
- family holidays
- school events or excursions
- your favourite pet
- beautiful scenery
- secret hideouts
- your friends
- flowers
- buskers
- lizards
- boats.

The list of possible photos is endless. The only limit is your imagination and energy!

YOUR CAMERA AND YOU

You've bought or borrowed a camera. Can you control it, or will it control you?

Practise looking through your camera, keeping it level. Hold your breath and gently squeeze the shutter button . . .

click!

Experiment with ways of holding your camera. (Why not practise with an empty camera to save film?) Which position suits you best? Get to know the feel of the shutter, so that you know just when it will fire.

Hold your camera with your elbows in, stand with your feet apart and lean against something if you feel wobbly. Try sitting, kneeling, or lying—but always stay steady.

Find a full-length mirror. Stand in front of it with your camera and study your reflection through the camera. Are you swaying?

Relax!

Try to keep still.

YOUR CAMERA AND YOU

You have a camera, you've bought some film, now study your camera's instruction booklet to learn how to load it. If you're uncertain, ask an adult to help you or go back to your camera shop. (Some cameras take 110 cartridges, but most take 35mm cassettes.)

Load your camera away from bright light, in a clean, dust-free place. Before loading the film, use a small air-brush to blow out any dust specks from the back of your camera. Always close the camera back gently but firmly.

Professional photographers often have to load film in very difficult situations.

Try some fun film loading:
- behind your back
- in a dark room
- with one hand
- blindfolded!

Your camera is loaded, you're ready to go . . . what can you photograph?

Let's change that around. What can you **not** take photos of?
Nothing!

Well, almost nothing, except:
• the teeth of snarling dogs
• teachers in a rage
• harassed parents
• crocodiles' eyes
• invisible UFOs
• music.

Look through magazines for photos and cut out your favourites: pin them onto a board. Find some old photograph albums and look at what people once photographed. Explore your local area and make a list of interesting things to photograph, note places you would like to return to.

YOUR CAMERA AND YOU

Finding inspiration

New places are full of things to discover and photograph, but so are very familiar places:

- your backyard
- the school playground
- the local shopping centre
- a fire station
- nearby parks
- your street.

Try photographing:

- friends
- fireworks
- petals
- pianists
- trees
- treasure
- clouds
- clocks
- babies
- bubbles
- dogs
- dragons.

How interesting can you make your photos?
Go to unusual places.
Look for different things.
Take photos at different times of day.
Above all, avoid taking endless photos of the same thing!

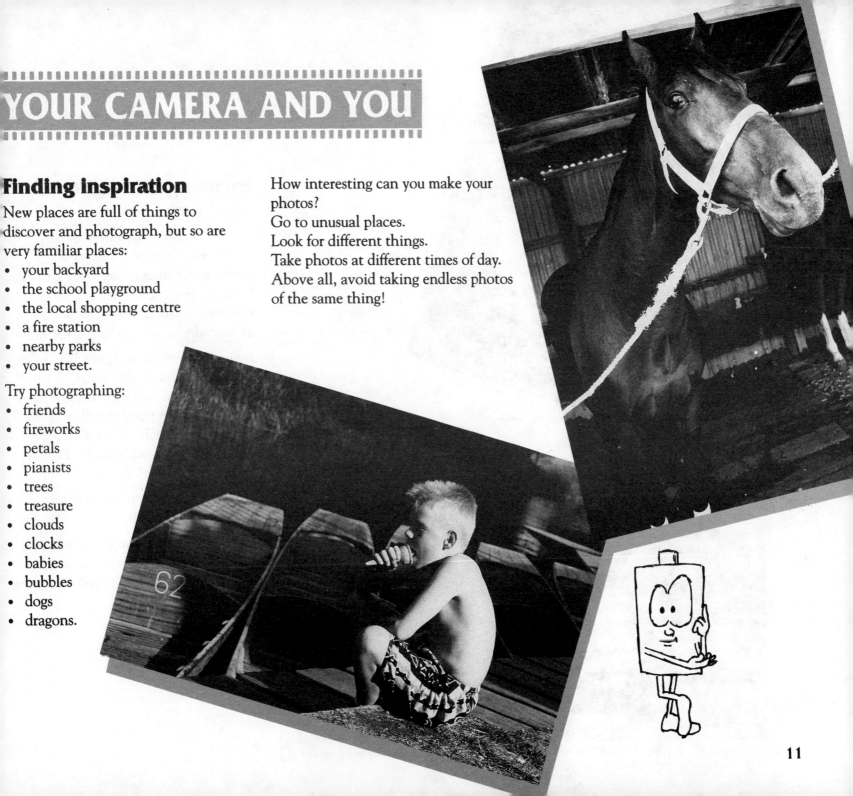

Focusing and light readings

Some cameras focus automatically, however far away the subject is positioned. Other cameras have to be focused on the main subject. Your camera's instruction booklet will explain if you have to focus, and how.

Some cameras can only use 100 ASA film, but most can use any ASA film. Matching your camera's ASA number to a film's ASA number tells your camera how much light a particular film needs. (Always remember to set your camera's ASA dial.)

How much light actually exists is something different.

There is most light on a sunny day. Less on an overcast day. And least of all on a dark, stormy day (not counting nights!).

YOUR CAMERA AND YOU

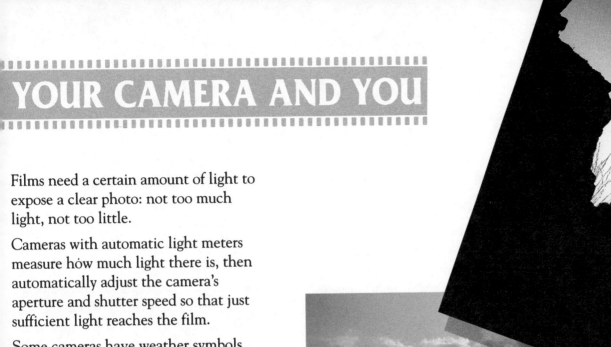

Films need a certain amount of light to expose a clear photo: not too much light, not too little.

Cameras with automatic light meters measure how much light there is, then automatically adjust the camera's aperture and shutter speed so that just sufficient light reaches the film.

Some cameras have weather symbols such as a bright sun, a light cloud, a storm cloud, and the photographer has to adjust the camera's weather dial for the actual conditions.

Other cameras with shutter-speed and aperture settings are more complicated. The speeds are fractions of a second, but are marked as 60, 125, 250 (really, 1/60, 1/125, 1/250). The apertures are marked as 'f-stops', eg 8, 11, 16. These cameras measure the actual light, but the photographer has to adjust the shutter and aperture settings.

13

Caring kids care for cameras

Cameras, especially cheap ones, are easily damaged. Always handle your camera carefully. Look after your camera and it should last for years.

Long-life camera clues

Operate your camera gently. If something jams, don't force it. You've probably made a mistake, so check your camera's instruction booklet.

Protect your camera from dust, knocks and rain by keeping it in its case. Use your camera's neck or wrist straps to save dropping it.

Cover your camera's lens with a clear, screw-on 'skylight' filter and keep the lens cap on, unless you are taking photos.

If the lens is smudged, clean it by huffing on it and then gently wiping it with a soft tissue. Remove any dust from the lens or camera back with a soft air-brush.

The end is nigh

Films have 12, 24 or 36 exposures or photographs on a roll. If your wind-on lever jams, check to see if you've finished your film. Some cameras automatically rewind each finished film, but others have to be rewound by hand.

Every time you take a photo, film is exposed by light, but to make negatives your film has to be developed. Prints can then be made from the negatives.

Try developing and printing your own black-and-white photos—it's fun (see pages 50–57). But until you know how, or if you are using colour film, take your completed films to a camera shop for developing and printing.

15

GOOD, BETTER, BEST PHOTOS

Now you know the basics of photography you can start taking better photos.

Don't worry if your first photos aren't very good. You'll get better with practice—and with self-criticism.

Start a photography notebook.

Record each photo you take: where it was taken, the time of day, the weather, and your camera settings. When your photos are printed decide which are best, and why. Check back to see how you took them.

You'll be amazed how your photos improve when you keep a record of them.

Pin your better photos onto a noticeboard, ordering them from best to not-so-good. Replace your 'best' photos as you improve. Throw away the real failures, but only after deciding why they don't work.

Over-exposed photo.

Under-exposed photo.

16

GOOD, BETTER, BEST PHOTOS

Some common problems

Blurry photos are caused by movement (or poor focusing).
Keep your camera as still as possible and squeeze the shutter gently. Use speeds above 1/125 if your subject is moving.

An out-of-focus photo.
Focus on the main subject, and don't get too close.
Over-exposed photos are caused by too much light entering the camera.
Check your ASA setting, and (unless your camera is automatic) check your light settings.

Dark photos are under-exposed, as not enough light has reached the film.
Check ASA and light settings.

Place your eye close to the viewfinder, to make sure you are seeing what the camera is pointing at. Keep your eye there till the shutter clicks. Watch out for wobbly horizons.

Out-of-focus photo.

Wobbly horizon—girl's knee is cut off.

Correctly exposed and focused photo.

17

A fly on the wall

The better you know a place, the better your photos will be.

Take a walk around your neighbourhood and observe its life. What's going on? Who are the interesting characters? What makes them interesting? Introduce yourself, get to know them. If they're friendly ask if you can return to photograph them later.

Everyone sees the world differently. Your photos are your record of how you see the world.

The more you look, the better you'll see!

Photographing without film is fun! Go on some expeditions looking for good photos. Practise taking lots of different 'photos', especially of moving things.

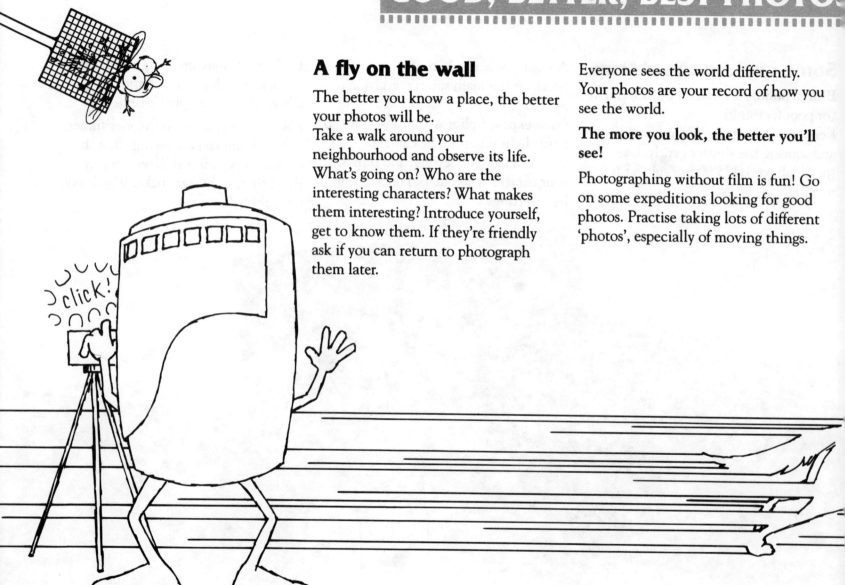

18

GOOD, BETTER, BEST PHOTOS

Head off to a place where you know things happen, find somewhere comfortable—wait and watch.

Patience makes great photos.

By waiting for unusual happenings to occur, and judging just the right moment to press the shutter, you will turn your ordinary photos into extraordinary ones.

Wait until:
- an old man lights his pipe
- a mother kisses her baby
- an old dog stretches
- a rainbow appears
- a boat capsizes
- the sun sets.

You'll soon develop a sense of timing: predicting when things will happen—and being ready to photograph them. The less conspicuous you are the better your photos will be.

MAGIC MOMENTS

Ever wondered how unusual photos were taken? The secret is often . . . just a trick or two.

Have some fun. Try taking photos like these with your friends. See if other people can work out how you took them, then think of some tricks yourself.

How big is the multi-coloured girl, and how small is her fairy friend? Distance, and who stood where were the secrets behind this photo.

Shop windows make interesting reflections. Choose a corner and you'll be cut in half.

Ever wondered how crazy mirrors work? Find some curved, shiny objects such as car hub-caps and start clicking! Visit a funfair, and photograph yourself in front of some really crazy mirrors.

Find a friend with four legs, but only two arms. Or someone with four arms and only two legs. (Or two heads and one body!)

Find a car window, or any other window, and have some fun! Experiment with reflections, or with people just looking odd behind glass.

Has the miner struck diamonds? Underexpose your photos, and you will be able to arrange your photo so that the Sun is shining through a small hole (such as between the miner's arm and his body), the sunlight will scatter to form a star. (Never look directly at the Sun.)

Try 'double exposing' photos, by taking two shots on the same piece of film. (Check your camera's instruction booklet to find out how.)

Hold Cellophane paper in front of your lens and take photos with strange colours.

21

DISPLAY YOUR PHOTOS

Now you've taken lots of photos, how about sharing them with your family and friends?

Most people enjoy looking at photos, especially if they're presented in a clear and interesting way.

Photograph albums come in all shapes, sizes—and prices. Why not arrange your photographs in cheaper, spiral-bound drawing books or loose-leaf folders? Arrange your photos by time, place, or theme. (Avoid a confusing jumble.) Vary the way you position photos, so that each page is slightly different. Add interesting captions and dates.

Make a 'rogues gallery': pin your favourite photos onto a board for people to see. Don't forget your candid shots—the ones some people wish you hadn't taken.

Montages are fun! Collect some poor photos and cut around their main subjects. Paste them onto cardboard backing to create a large, montage picture.

Show your photos:
• in albums
• on display boards
• as montages
• in storybooks
• on cards
• with cartoons
• in slide shows
• with mats
• in frames.

22

DISPLAY YOUR PHOTOS

Make a book with a series of photo stories. Arrange your photos in order, paste them into your book—then add captions to highlight your photos' contents.

Make your own greeting cards. It's fun and you'll save money! Select some favourite photos, get some thick paper, scissors and paste. Cut the paper to slightly more than twice the size of the photo, fold it in half—and paste on your photo.

Cartoon crazy? Select some funny photos, carefully cut out speech-balloons for them, then paste the photos onto coloured paper or cardboard. Fill the speech-balloons with cryptic comments.

Have a slide night. Arrange a slide show for your family and friends to show them your colour photos. But beware . . . slide shows can easily become very boring. Arrange the room as you want it beforehand and test the projector. Only show your very best photos, don't show too many, and have your photos arranged in some order—and avoid talking too much!

Making a mask, or 'mat', adds impact to photos, and can be used to hide any unwanted edges. Your very, very best photos deserve to have mats, and if you can afford them—frames.

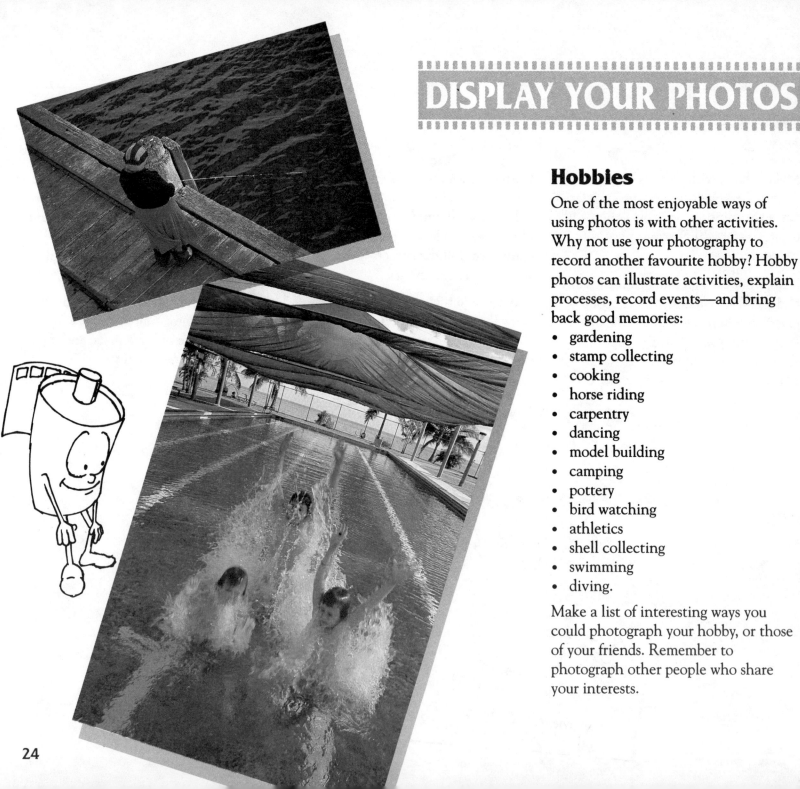

Hobbies

One of the most enjoyable ways of using photos is with other activities. Why not use your photography to record another favourite hobby? Hobby photos can illustrate activities, explain processes, record events—and bring back good memories:

- gardening
- stamp collecting
- cooking
- horse riding
- carpentry
- dancing
- model building
- camping
- pottery
- bird watching
- athletics
- shell collecting
- swimming
- diving.

Make a list of interesting ways you could photograph your hobby, or those of your friends. Remember to photograph other people who share your interests.

24

GOING HIKING?

Head for the country—and you'll discover some wonderful photo opportunities. You might begin by photographing the people you're with, or the places where you stop: lookouts, lunch breaks, overnight camps. Then there are all the plants, insects and animals. And don't forget the land itself.

You can take great landscape photos with even a simple camera, but it takes time and lots of patience. Resist the temptation to grab snapshots of every attractive view you see. Instead,

look,

think,

decide.

Is there a better view nearby? Will the light improve later on? What patterns or textures are there? Does anything show the landscape's size? (A boulder? A tree?) Should the horizon be high or low? (Is the land or sky most interesting?)

Great landscape photos emphasise one main feature.

MORE WAYS TO USE YOUR PHOTOS

Neighbourhood shops often have noticeboards. Ask if you can display your photos. Become an environmental watchdog, posting up photos of local black spots and of people who have improved your area. Record any significant local events and pin up your photos.

Keen on sports? Why not photograph some local teams during their training sessions and matches? You'll soon get to know the players, and perhaps sell some photos!

Old people often live alone. Get to know some of your local 'oldies'. Their faces are usually full of character and they have time to pose for portraits. They'll be delighted if you offer to give them photos to send to their families.

Professional photographers often began their careers by photographing their local areas—its places, characters, and events. When you start taking really good photos, why not contact your local newspaper? They might publish some of your photos.

School projects

Photography is a great way to make school projects interesting—and fun.

Talk with your teachers and friends, use your imagination and you'll soon discover countless ways to use photos to add to your school subjects.

Read as much as possible about the subject of your project, then think about what photos you can take to illustrate your work.

Remember to publish your photos: in project books, on noticeboards, with slide presentations.

Clubs and magazines

Does your school have a photography club and a magazine or newspaper? If it hasn't, don't assume no-one else is interested. Get together with some friends, find a helpful teacher and start the ball rolling.

A photograph is worth a thousand words

Even single photos can 'say' a lot, and collections of photos tell us even more. Look through some magazines, such as *National Geographic*, and you'll see how photos can tell wonderful stories.

Try making some photo stories:
- a day in the life of . . .
- the school excursion
- my favourite sport
- building a cubby
- spring flowers
- flying kites
- pollution
- Christmas.

Exciting photo stories use related pictures to tell a story. Begin with some introductory, 'scene-setting' photos. Then take a series of photos giving the story's details—whether it's about a place, an event or a journey.

Later, edit (or select) the very best photos and arrange them in order. Finally, write some interesting captions to help other people enjoy your story.

It was a hot, windy day in Googong . . .

FIRE DANGER TODAY

LOW MODERATE HIGH VERY HIGH EXTREME

TOTAL FIRE BAN — NO FIRES

GOOGONG FORESHORES CLOSED

Bushfire! The firefighting teams were quickly on their way.

Now for some daydreaming . . . daydreaming?

You've probably often been told not to daydream. After all, daydreaming is a bad habit.

Correction!

Some of the world's most original inventions, and some of civilisation's most creative art, are the result of daydreaming—of letting the mind wander.

Try letting your mind relax, push away all the trivial thoughts that tend to clog up your thinking box . . . who knows what great photos your mind's eye might imagine.

Feed your imagination, and you'll develop an original way of seeing. Blindfold yourself! Then imagine 'mind pictures' of everything in your room . . . in your house . . . on a desert island. Practise this regularly, and you'll soon start seeing things you had never noticed before.

The smoke hung over the blackened bush.

They had to stop the fire spreading through the bush.

It was hot, dangerous work, but at last the fire was out.

MAGIC SILVER—FILM

Films are made up of microscopic silver crystals. Millions of them would barely cover your fingertip. And, when stuck onto long strips of very thin gelatine, they make—film.

Some films record colour pictures, but some only show black-and-white images. The silver crystals are the film's light-sensitive emulsion. Film emulsion is changed (or exposed) when light hits it. To make the change visible and permanent, the film is then put into a liquid developer. Hey presto—a negative.

Negatives are 'halfway' photos. Photographic paper, like film, is covered with tiny light-sensitive crystals. If light is shone through a negative onto photographic paper, the paper is affected (exposed). When it's developed, the changes become visible. Abracadabra—a photograph.

Some films react more quickly than others. 'Fast' films, such as 400 ASA, only need a little light. 'Slow' films, such as 64 ASA, have fewer, smaller crystals and need more light than fast films. The best films to use are medium-speed films, between 100–200 ASA.

Object

Negative

Positive

Now for some fun!

Visit your local camera shop, and buy some photographic paper, developer and fixer. Read the chemicals' instructions, then carefully mix them with water.

Find a fern leaf or some other interesting, flat shape. Take it into a very dark room with the photographic paper. Remove a sheet of photographic paper, close the packet, then tape your shape onto the paper's glossy emulsion side. Leave the paper in the sunlight for a day, then remove the shape.

Surprised?

In a darkened room take out a sheet of photographic paper, then close the packet. Go into a brightly lit room with your sheet, and paint shapes onto the paper's glossy side with developer.

What happens?

To keep your pictures, dip them in the fixer, then wash and dry them.

Go into a darkened room and tape some interesting shapes, such as a fern leaf, onto sheets of photographic paper. Take them into bright light. Back in the darkened room, develop and fix the images.

Can you think of other ways to experiment with photographic paper and developer?

Colour or black-and-white?

Some photographers always use colour film. Others prefer black-and-white film. And some use both.

Choosing between colour or black-and-white is up to you.

Flick through some magazines, and cut out some colour and black-and-white photos that catch your eye. Which do you prefer, or are they just different?

Make a display or montage of your cut-outs, one for colour, one for black-and-white.

Try turning your black-and-white photos into colour photos by colouring them with felt-tip pens. After all, the first colour photos were coloured, or tinted, by hand.

MAGIC SILVER—FILM

Go outside and look around. What do you see?

Colours or shapes?

Colour photos give a very good general impression of a scene. The best colour photos are often quite simple, with only one or two main colours.

Black-and-white photos are better at showing shapes and shades of light, and are often best for special light effects.

Black-and-white film has another great advantage: it's easy to learn how to develop and print it at home (see pages 50–56).

Colour developing and printing is very complicated, so few photographers do colour processing at home. If you wish to project photos, you must use colour-slide film.

PHOTOGRAPHING PEOPLE

Are any two people exactly alike?

Look in a mirror, then study the faces of people you know.

Portraits, or photos of individuals, are more than just snapshots. Good portraits tell us something about a person: their character, moods and lifestyle.

Get to know people before trying to photograph them, and ask where they would like to be photographed. The best portraits are generally taken when people are surrounded by the things they care about:

- a gardener amongst shrubs and flowers
- a yachtie aboard their boat
- a writer with their books
- a toddler playing.

Take your time. People generally relax if they're doing something, and if you talk to them quietly from behind your camera. (Don't fuss!) Wait to capture natural, spontaneous expressions.

You'll need to take several photos to get one really good portrait, as people's expressions change very quickly. Make sure to avoid direct sunlight which causes harsh face shadows.

Self-portraits

Try photographing yourself!

Look for reflections to photograph yourself in: mirrors, car bodies, hub-caps, water, or any other shiny objects. Flat surfaces, such as mirrors, give true reflections, but curved surfaces, such as hub-caps, make funny, distorted ones.

If your camera has a self-timer (a delayed-action shutter), place the camera facing you, set the self-timer—and race into the picture! If your camera can take a cable release, attach one, smile and—squeeze!

Click!

This is your life!

How about collecting all the old photos of yourself you can find? Arrange them in chronological order, and stick them onto a long concertina of paper. Leave room for more!

THE SHADES OF LIGHT

Have an adventure! Go to a favourite place early one morning with a friend, your camera, a notebook and some food. Take photos every half-hour of one view, and write down how the light changes during the day. Compare the photos later!

Photography means 'drawing with light'. Natural light changes constantly with the seasons, the weather, and the time of day. Study light's different moods and your photos will soon be stunning.

On a fine day, early morning light is warm and cheerful. Midday light is harsh and glary, with short, dark shadows. Late afternoon light is very dramatic, with yellowish light sometimes turning to glowing gold just before sunset.

Light overcast days have a bright, white light. Dull overcast days are dark and gloomy. And misty days have a pearly light—mysterious and beautiful.

Keep an umbrella handy—rainy days often have wonderful light!

THE SHADES OF LIGHT

Back-lit photo.

Cross-lit photo.

Front-lit photo.

Whenever you go outside, notice how the light looks. Check the weather and the time of day.

You'll soon be able to predict how the light will probably be, although you can never actually control it.

But you can control how you use light.

Making the best use of available light turns ordinary photos into extraordinary ones.

Front-lit photos have the sunlight shining directly onto the subject, so there are no shadows. This works better in colour than black-and-white, but can be rather uninteresting.

Cross-lit photos have the sunlight shining sideways across them, creating fascinating shadows that highlight surface textures.

Back-lit photos can be very dramatic, but they're very difficult to expose correctly.

Planning your photos is the secret to taking great pictures. Decide how to use the best light, and plan an effective composition.

Composition

Good photos stand out because each part of the photo contributes to the overall effect. Composition is about arranging the shapes in a photo so it 'works'.

Find a piece of cardboard, and cut it to make a frame. The frame's proportions should be similar to your camera's viewfinder.

Now, practise taking 'photos' with your frame. Wander around, looking for interesting subjects. Use your frame to select **what** you want to photograph, then use it to decide **how** to compose or arrange your photo.

Subject centred, with back-ground contributing to photo without dominating it.

ALL SHAPES AND SIZES

Decide what you want **in** your photos, and try to keep everything else **out.**

Make your main subjects big and bold, to show them clearly. Move backwards and forwards to judge the best size for your main subject.

Avoid having distracting things near the edges of your photos, or in the middle of them! Move position slightly to remove unwanted objects. Try to keep the backgrounds of photos simple.

Browse through some books and magazines, checking the composition of photos. What can you learn? Try sketching some imaginary 'photos' to get your composition going. By drawing interesting arrangements of simple shapes like circles, squares and rectangles you will learn about composition, as most actual objects have outlines similar to these shapes.

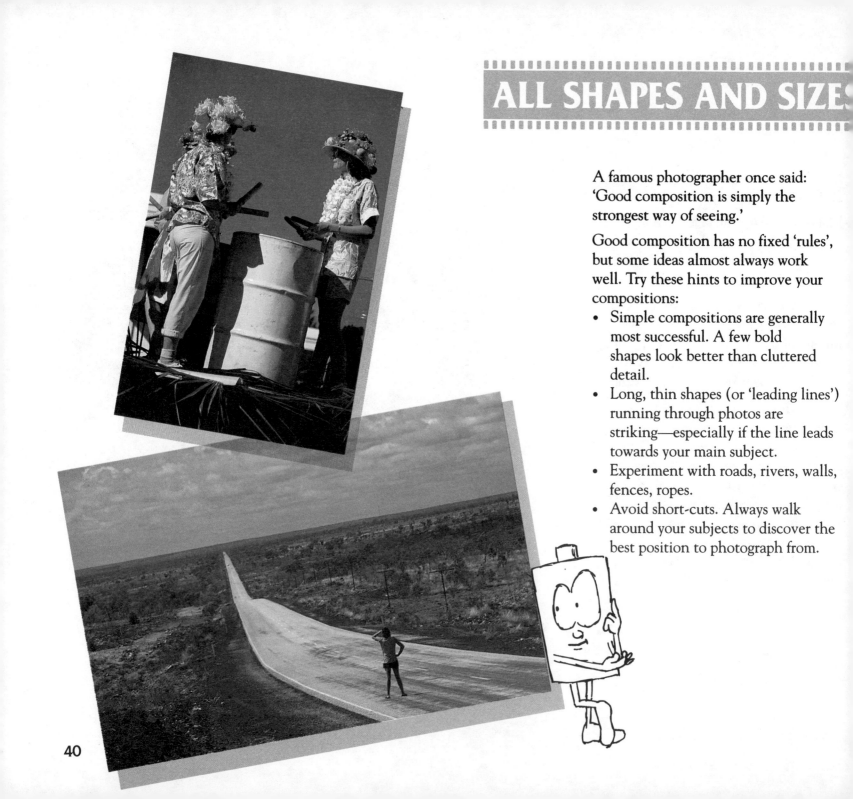

A famous photographer once said: 'Good composition is simply the strongest way of seeing.'

Good composition has no fixed 'rules', but some ideas almost always work well. Try these hints to improve your compositions:

- Simple compositions are generally most successful. A few bold shapes look better than cluttered detail.
- Long, thin shapes (or 'leading lines') running through photos are striking—especially if the line leads towards your main subject.
- Experiment with roads, rivers, walls, fences, ropes.
- Avoid short-cuts. Always walk around your subjects to discover the best position to photograph from.

More ideas for interesting compositions

Divide your composition frame into thirds, and paste string along the divisions. Now look for more 'photos', and decide where your main subjects should be. It's hard to say why, but photos often look best when the main subject is near the intersection of the imaginary 'thirds' lines.

Try using windows, doors, overhanging trees or archways to 'frame' or surround your main subject—so drawing attention to it.

Photos looking up or down, from very low or very high positions, are often extremely interesting. Crouch down, stand on car roofs, climb hills (and get some good boots!).

Think about where the horizon line should be. Remember you can turn your camera sideways for vertical photos of long, tall shapes like trees or chimneys.

Try arranging repeated shapes, to give a sense of 'rhythm'—or arrange shapes to 'balance' each other.

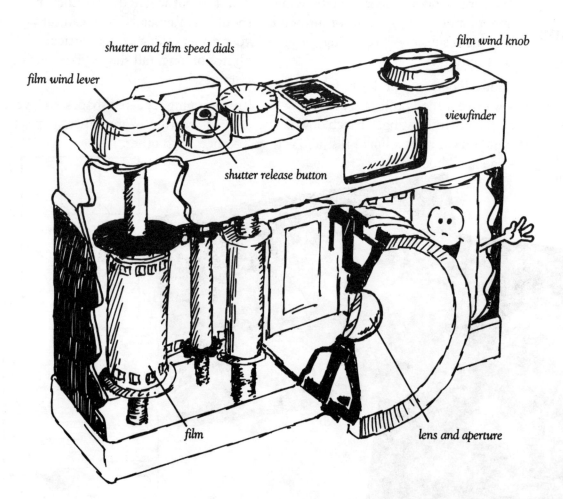

film wind lever

shutter and film speed dials

film wind knob

viewfinder

shutter release button

film

lens and aperture

The first true photos were made ab
150 years ago. Photography became
popular about 50 years later when
George Eastman designed a small
camera—the Kodak.

'You press the button, we do the res
Eastman boasted of his simple came
and people rushed to buy them.

Cameras have come a long way sinc
then, but modern cameras still have
things in common with with the m
loved Kodak:
- a light-proof box
- a lens
- a shutter
- an aperture
- a film plane
- a viewfinder.

The lens focuses the light. The shut
like your eyelids, is a 'door'. When i
opens, even for a split-second, light
floods into the camera. The aperture
like the iris in your eye, helps contro
how much light enters the camera.
film plane keeps the film flat, and th
viewfinder helps you point the came

...ying your camera

...n today's simplest cameras would
...e delighted George Eastman, and
...most complicated ones would have
...zed him.

...t some camera shops and collect
...ous camera brochures. Ask about
...four most common kinds of camera:
... 10 cartridge cameras
...ocket cameras
...5mm compact cameras
...5mm single-lens-reflex cameras
...SLRs).

...ou're a beginner, you'll learn most
...ut photography with a simple
...era (although 110 cameras are
...er limiting.) So, unless you've
...ady used a basic camera, buy an
...xpensive one first. Save your money
...uy a better camera when you know
...re about photography.

Get to know your camera

Check your camera's instruction
booklet, then experiment with your
camera's knobs and dials. Blindfold
yourself, and learn to feel your camera's
controls without thinking. The more
you understand your camera, the better
your photos will be.

43

DRAWING WITH LIGHT

Interesting photos can be taken in countless ways:

- in colour
- in black-and-white
- from windows
- underwater
- quickly
- slowly
- at midday
- by moonlight.

Good photographers, however, all have something in common: they understand how light makes photos.

That isn't surprising!

Photography (photo–graphy), remember, means 'drawing with light'. Light, and the things it shows, come and go. But film can capture moments of light, 'freezing' events on photographs forever.

DRAWING WITH LIGHT

Light rays travel out from sources of light, such as the Sun or a candle. Light also travels out from objects which reflect light.

Find a flashlight, and go into a very dark closet with a friend—or into an unlit room at night. What can you see? Turn on the flashlight: what can you see now?

White objects reflect all light rays. Coloured things reflect some light. Black objects reflect no light at all.

Bending light

Your eyes and brain are your most important photographic equipment!

Unlike a camera, your eyes can't record 'pictures' permanently, although your brain can recall past sights. But, like cameras, your eyes refract light.

Refraction

Stand a pencil in a glass of water. Does it appear bent? Is it **really** bent? As light passes from water to air, or vice versa, it is bent—or refracted.

Glass also refracts light. And, if it's shaped into a curved, convex lens, glass can bend light to form a clear image (or picture). Hold a magnifying glass (a simple lens) near a piece of white cardboard. Can you make an image on the cardboard by moving the magnifying glass in and out?

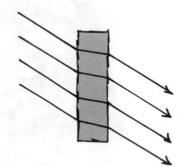

Glass bends, or refracts, light.

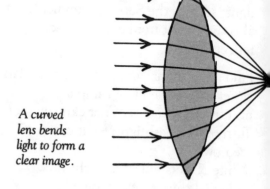

A curved lens bends light to form a clear image.

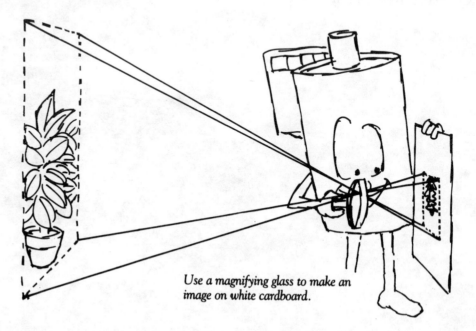

Use a magnifying glass to make an image on white cardboard.

46

DRAWING WITH LIGHT

Your eyes exposed

As light enters your eyes, their lenses refract light rays to focus them at the back of your eyes. Muscles change the lenses' shapes, depending on how far away you are looking. People whose eye lenses aren't working correctly need other lenses—glasses or contacts—to help their eyes focus clearly.

Your iris, the coloured ring around your pupils, allows the right amount of light to enter your eyes.

Go into a dark room, and study your irises in a mirror. Then go into bright sunlight, and look at your irises. Did they change size?

Irises expand in dim light to allow you to see clearly, and contract in bright light to prevent too much light entering your eyes.

An amazing fact: the 'pictures' formed on your retina are actually upside down! Your brain 'turns' the picture the right way up. Feeling giddy?

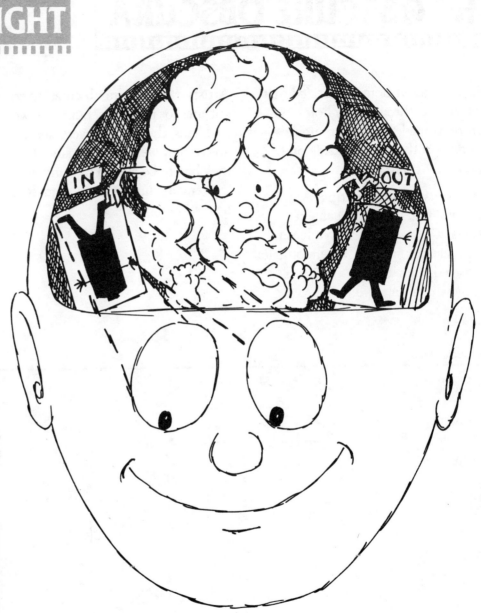

THE OBSCURE OBSCURA

Long ago, desert nomads noticed that light shining through tiny holes in their tents made dim, blurry images—or pictures—of the scene outside on the opposite tent wall.

People began experimenting. And, about 500 years ago, the 'camera obscura' was invented, with a lens to make a clearer image. 'Camera obscura' means 'a darkened room', which is exactly what they were.

Artists used 'camera obscuras' to trace outlines for paintings, but there were problems: the pictures were upside down, they were not permanent, so they had to be copied by hand, and 'camera obscuras' were extremely heavy.

A camera obscura.

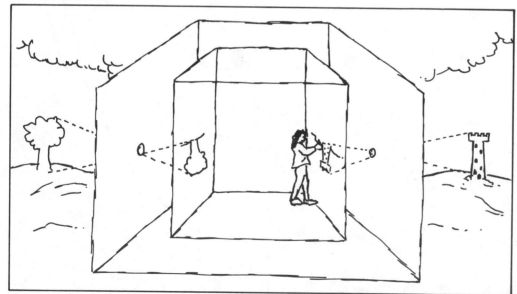

THROUGH A PINHOLE

Pinhole cameras, the very simplest cameras, are miniature 'camera obscuras' (without lenses).

To make one you'll need:

a small cardboard box
greaseproof paper
sticky tape
scissors
tinfoil and a pin.

What to do:

1 Cover the open end of your box with greaseproof paper.

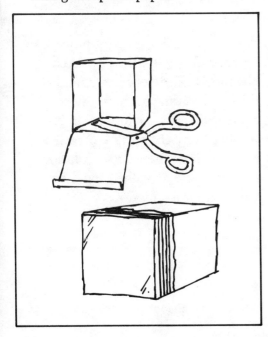

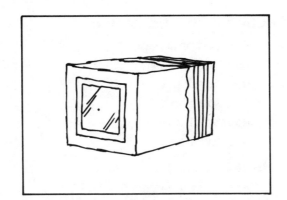

2 Cut a small hole in the centre of the opposite side, cover it with tinfoil and prick a hole in the foil.

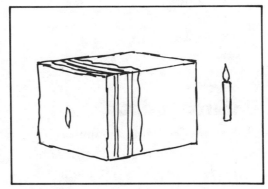

3 Ask an adult to light a candle in a darkened room.

Can you see a 'photo' of the candle on the greaseproof paper? Try using your pinhole camera to take other 'photos'.

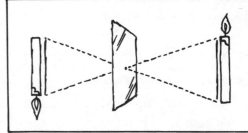

4 Make your pinhole larger. What happens to the 'photo'?

Ordinary cameras, and eyes, have lenses to bend light rays to produce a clear picture. Pinhole cameras don't have lenses, because the pinhole allows only one light ray from each point to enter the box—so making a reasonably clear, upside-down picture.

DEVELOPING AND PRINTING

Develop your own negatives, print your own photos—and you'll discover a magical world of interest and fun!

You'll also have more control over your photography. And if you take lots of photos, you'll save money in the long run.

Setting up a darkroom isn't cheap. Split the costs by finding a friend to share a darkroom, or join a camera club with its own darkroom. Second-hand equipment is worth investigating: check your local paper. Buy as many things as possible in ordinary stores, not camera shops—and you'll save heaps!

Essential equipment:
film-developing tank
3 measuring cylinders
thermometer (15°–30°C)
clock with a second hand
4 plastic trays, 20 x 30cm
safelight and white light
sheet of glass, 20 x 30cm
paper developer
empty plastic bottles
enlarger

Chemicals and paper:
photographic paper
paper developer
film developer
stop solution
fixer solution
negative files

Handy extras:
masking frame
focus finder
film clips
film wiper
print tongs
scissors
sticky tape
small funnel
a radio for company!

Darkroom details

Darkrooms can be set up almost anywhere. Laundries and bathrooms make ideal temporary darkrooms (if your family agrees!). Other possible spaces are cellars, partitioned-off sections of garages, even large cupboards. Running water isn't essential, and an area about 1 x 2 metres is just sufficient.

Darkrooms have to be blacked-out, so having small windows helps. Use black plastic to cut out any light. Even the tiniest glimmer can spoil your photos, so double-check that light isn't sneaking in. (And it can sneak!)

You'll need two areas, a 'dry' area and a 'wet' area. Keep the two areas as far apart as possible. Place your enlarger in the 'dry' area, and your trays for chemicals in the 'wet' area. You'll also need at least two lights: an ordinary white light, and an orange or red safelight.

When everything is ready, move your equipment in. Mix the powdered chemicals—developer, stop, and fixer—according to their instructions. Store these 'stock solutions' in clearly-labelled, air-tight bottles. (You may need to dilute these 'stock solutions' further before actually using them. Check their instructions.)

DEVELOPING AND PRINTING

1 Enlarger

2 Developer

3 Stop

4 Fixer

5 Thermometer

6 Tongs

7 Safelight

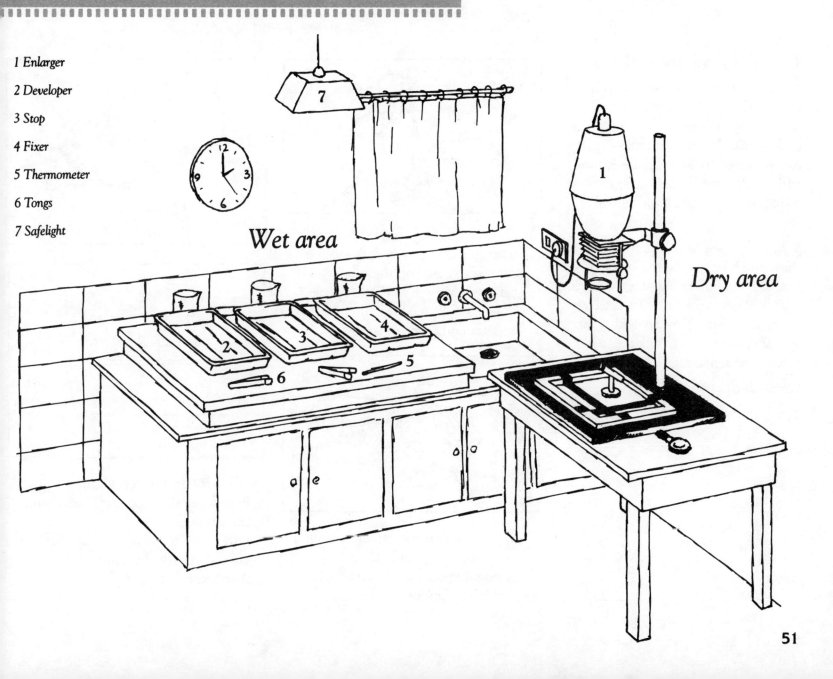

Wet area

Dry area

Developing negatives

Negatives have to be developed **in total darkness**. You'll need a developing tank (a kind of miniature darkroom). Developing tanks come in two styles: easily loaded, plastic tanks with ratchet spools, and more difficult to handle metal tanks with metal spools.

Whichever you have, ask someone to show you how to load the spool. Then find some old film, and practise loading it in daylight. (Take care to touch only the film's edges.) Now try with your eyes shut, and then in a darkened room. Don't give up!

Confident?

You're ready to develop your first film.

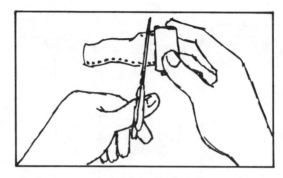

1 Cut off your film's angled leader, then go into a totally dark room or cupboard. Lever off the film cassette's top with a bottle opener, then carefully feed the film off the cassette and onto the spool.

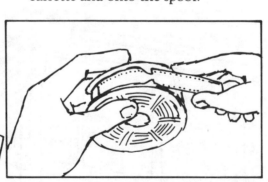

2 When the film is completely wound on, place the spool in the developing tank and push on the tank's lid. Turn on the light.

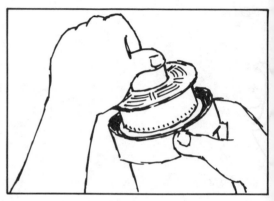

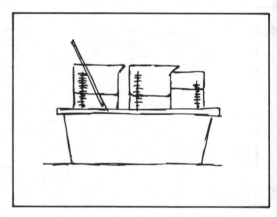

3 Fill three measuring cylinders with film developer, stop and fixer. Stand the cylinders in hot or icy water, to bring their temperatures to exactly 20° Centigrade. Use your thermometer to check.

6 Now pour the fixer into the tank. Agitate it briefly, then on and off for about a minute. Pour away the fixer after the recommended time.

7 Take off the tank's cap, and place the tank in a sink. Direct a gentle stream of water into the tank, and leave it there for half-an-hour. Don't be impatient! Poorly washed film is spotty.

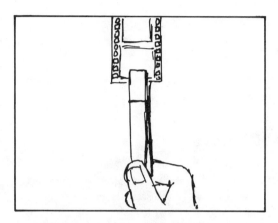

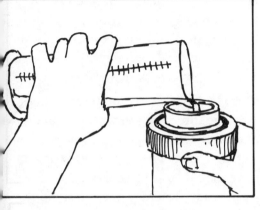

4 Check the time, then fill the tank with film developer. Replace the tank's cap, and agitate the tank vigorously for 15 seconds. Continue to agitate the tank according to the developer's instructions. Begin pouring out the developer just before the recommended time.

5 Pour the stop solution into the tank and agitate it gently for about a minute. Then pour the stop back into its container. (Unlike developer and fixer, stop solution can be reused.)

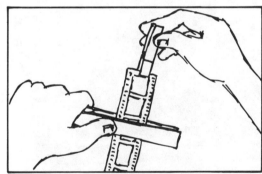

8 Attach a film clip (or clothes peg) to the film, and take it off the spool. Gently wipe the film with a film wiper to remove water drops, or wipe it with two fingers held like scissors.

9 Hang the film to dry in a clean place, with a clip or peg on the bottom to stop it curling. When it is quite dry, cut the negatives into strips of six photos and slide them into a paper negative file.

Printing photos

Your enlarger is your most important piece of darkroom equipment. It does what its name suggests—enlarges small negatives into much larger 'positive' prints (photos). When you buy an enlarger, make sure its frame is rigid and that it has a good lens. Before

enlarging your negatives, you need to make a sheet of contact prints. They'll help you decide which photos you want to take the time (and paper) to enlarge. Make sure you're prepared.

Plug the enlarger in, and test its lamp. Arrange three trays in your wet area, and fill them with paper developer, stop and fixer. The developer, stop and fixer should be kept at about 20° Centigrade. You may need to stand the trays in hot or icy water to adjust their temperature.

Always dry your hands before touching switches, negatives or paper.

1 Turn on the darkroom safelight. Place a piece of photographic paper, shiny side up, on the enlarger's base.

2 Cover the enlarger's lens with its red safety filter, and turn on the enlarger lamp. Shift the enlarger head until its light just covers the paper. Set the enlarger's aperture to 'f8'.

3 Place your negative strips shiny side up on the paper, then cover them with a piece of clear glass. Move the red safety filter away for seven seconds, exposing the negatives and paper to white light.

54

DEVELOPING AND PRINTING

4 Slide the paper, shiny side down, into the developer tray, and rock it gently. After about 30 seconds, turn the paper—your photos should be visible! Swish the developer gently, before removing the paper at the recommended time.

5 Place the paper in the stop solution for about 15 seconds, then transfer it to the fixer. Fix the paper for about two minutes, then turn on the white light.

6 Leave the print in the fixer for about 10 minutes, then wash it under running water for about 30 minutes. Dry your contact print by laying it on blotting paper, or hanging it up.

Excited?

If your contact print is too dark, make another with a shorter exposure time. If it's too light, you need a longer exposure. When you're satisfied with a contact print, study it carefully and decide which photos you'd like to enlarge first.

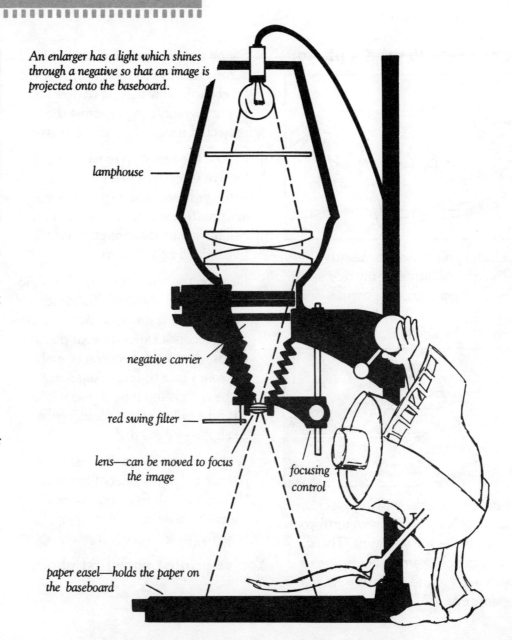

An enlarger has a light which shines through a negative so that an image is projected onto the baseboard.

lamphouse —

negative carrier

red swing filter —

lens—can be moved to focus the image

focusing control

paper easel—holds the paper on the baseboard

55

You're ready to print a photo:

1 Select a photo, find its negative, and place the negative (shiny side up) in the enlarger's negative carrier. Turn off the darkroom's white light and turn on the safelight.

2 Turn on the enlarger lamp, and move its head up or down until your photo is the size you want. Then focus the enlarger, either by eye or with a focus finder. Set the enlarger's aperture at 'f8'.

3 Swing the enlarger's red safety filter across, so only red light is hitting the baseboard. Now place a narrow strip of photographic paper across the projected image. This is a 'test strip'.

4 Expose the test strip to white light for five seconds. Then cover ¼ of it with cardboard and expose it for another five seconds. Continue until you have four sections exposed for five, 10, 15 and 20 seconds.

5 Develop the test strip, just as you did the contact print. After fixing it, examine the test strip to decide how many seconds exposure your photo needs. (It may be between one of the four times or longer or shorter. If the time is too long or too short alter the enlarger). It shouldn't be too light—or too dark.

6 When you're sure of the best time, put the enlarger's safety filter across, lay out a full sheet of photographic paper—expose it, then develop, stop, fix, wash and dry it.

You've printed your first photo.

DEVELOPING AND PRINTING

Improving your prints

To make really good prints you'll need more information—and lots of practice! Here are some pointers:

Tones and contrast

You can choose whether to make your prints on glossy or matt photographic paper. Whichever you prefer, you must also decide whether to use normal (grade 2), soft (grade 1) or hard (grade 3) paper for individual prints.

Find a 2B pencil! Try to shade shapes on white paper which cover the entire range from very light grey, to middle greys, through to extremely dark greys. Good prints should include a full range of these shades or 'tones' of grey: from spots of pure white, through all the greys, to small areas that are inky black.

Make your first prints on grade 2 paper. Then, if your prints have too much contrast, with very dark shadows but no details in the lighter areas, make better prints using soft (grade 1) paper. Or, if a print is too 'flat', with mid-greys but no blacks or whites, make a second print on hard (grade 3) paper. (If your negatives are always very 'flat' or 'contrasty', find out about varying your film exposure and development.)

Dodging and burning

Improve your prints further (and have some fun) by 'dodging' and 'burning in'. If your shadow areas are too dark, 'dodge' them by shading them with a piece of cardboard on a wire handle while your print is being exposed. If your light areas are still too pale, after exposing the main photo 'burn in' the pale areas with more light exposure —meanwhile shading the rest of the photo with cardboard. (Always keep the cardboard moving slightly when dodging or burning in.)

ADVANCED PHOTOGRAPHY

If you've made it to here, and have tried most of the activities, you're well along the way to taking great photos.

But there's still lots more to learn!

This last section on more advanced photography provides food for thought—and for further experimenting. If you're keen to learn more about photography (and we've only scratched the surface!) pick up some hints here and head for your local library.

Are you controlling your camera or is it controlling you?

Simple cameras are ideal to begin with, but they're manufactured to automatically produce 'standard' photos. Improving your photos means learning how to take 'non-standard' photos: photos where you're controlling your camera, not vice versa. If you've been using a pocket camera, you might move on to a 35mm compact camera.

With a better lens, and some control over exposure, your photos should improve. However, if you're really keen, consider buying a 35mm single-lens-reflex camera. SLRs are light, extremely versatile, and (if you choose a manual/auto model) you're in full control. Visit some camera shops, and check their SLRs and compacts. Take your time . . . the more you look the happier you'll be!

ADVANCED PHOTOGRAPHY

Lenses

Take a chair outside your house and put it in a position where it appears larger than the house. Walk away: does the chair still appear larger than the house? Experiment with other different-sized objects. Distance alters perspective, or the way we see objects. However, our brains cleverly reorganise what our eyes actually see, so we think chairs are always smaller than houses. Unlike people, camera lenses can't think. By using different lenses you'll discover an exciting new world.

The best reason for buying an SLR camera is that SLRs can be used with different lenses. Human eyes always see a viewing angle of about 45 degrees, but different SLR lenses are designed to 'see' almost any angle—and so you can select the perspective you want.

The most common lenses are:
- standard lenses, covering about 45°
- wide-angle lenses, covering between 60°–90°
- telephoto lenses, ranging from about 30°–2°
- zoom lenses, which change their angle of view.

Don't expect instant results with a new lens. You'll need time and practice to see the way the lens does.

18mm/94°
24mm/84°
35mm/62°
50mm/46°
85mm/29°
135mm/18°
200mm/12°
400mm/6°
1000mm/2.5°

59

Self-taught photographers

Photography is extremely complicated. It's a strange mixture of chemistry and art, full of mysterious, baffling techniques that only famous photographers ever really understand.

True or false?

False!

Advanced photography is mostly quite easily understood. The only secrets are: thinking, experimenting . . . and time. Perhaps that's why so many great photographers taught themselves: by reading, by practising, by looking.

Decode these technical clues to taking better photographs.

Definition Relax! Definition isn't about how sharp your vocabulary is, just how sharp your shots are. Banish camera shake, buy a tripod.

Depth of field might be about gardening, but it also shows how much of a photo is in focus. Small apertures and wide lenses make it deeper.

Available light is the only available light. Find a tripod, and wait for some stunningly beautiful colours.

Flash photography. It's artificial, but handy. Many cameras have built-in flashes, but most SLR's need separate flash units.

ADVANCED PHOTOGRAPHY

Tripods have three legs and countless uses. They can improve definition, extend depth of field, and even improve composition. Telephoto-lenses love tripods!

Incident light isn't reflected light, but reflected light was once incident light. The difference can make or break exposures (and your heart!).

Grain has nothing to do with wheat, but it's similar to sand. Film speeds and developers affect grain. Some people think grainy photos are great, others dislike them.

Filters are moody transformers. They can turn hills blue and seas blood-red. Polarisers are really intense (and extremely useful!).

Contrast is to do with light and colours. It can be extreme, as with pandas, or barely exist at all, as on koalas.

Bracketing is what colour photographers do when they're uncertain about the light. Hedge your bets: bracket, bracket, bracket.

Stopping action a few tricks and you can make fast-moving objects pin-sharp—or blur them completely to suggest speed. Panning (but not for gold) is where to begin.

61

You the camera

To return to the beginning: your 'seeing eye', your mind and eyes working together, is your most valuable photographic equipment. However complicated your camera (and some have too many gadgets!) it's your 'seeing eye', not your camera, that decides how to take photos. Some people with extremely expensive cameras take very ordinary photos.

The best photos reflect years of persistence.

The more you know about photography, the more you can learn by looking at good photos—and thinking how they were taken. Read camera magazines, and study good photos and paintings to feed your 'seeing eye'.

Free your imagination and strengthen your powers of observation. Practise the 'visualising' exercise on page 29 regularly, and try to imagine increasingly complex scenes.

Find out about different kinds of photography: news, documentary, landscape, portraiture, advertising, fashion, art and scientific. Which interests you most?

Start an 'advanced' photographic notebook. Jot down methods and results, successes and failures, places to visit, ideas for photos.

Above all, believe in yourself.

Enjoy your photography, but don't allow your camera to rule your life! Leave it behind sometimes, and let the world's beauty (and ugliness) touch your heart. Remember: great photographers were once all beginners. Find out about their lives—be inspired!

Famous photographers say:

'Good seeing doesn't ensure good photographs, but good photographs are impossible without it. The art of seeing is the art of photography.'
Freeman Patterson

'You put your camera around your neck in the morning along with your shoes, and there it is, sharing your life with you. The camera is an instrument that teaches people to see without a camera.'
Dorothea Lange

'Getting up at dawn on a winter morning and driving around searching for photographs is a chilly but wonderful experience.'
Ansel Adams

'Often while travelling with our camera we arrive just as the Sun slips over the horizon of a wonderful moment, too late to expose a photo, but time enough to expose our hearts.'
Minor White

READING LIST

The more you read, the better your photos will be!

Beginner books:

Me and my camera by Joe Partridge, Ash and Grant, 1981.

Everyone's book of photography by Don Morley, Optimum Books, 1982.

The young photographer's handbook by George Haines, Hamlyn, 1982.

Snap! Photography for beginners by Christopher Wright, Puffin Books, 1979.

Flying start photography by Keith Wicks, Sampson Low, 1979.

More advanced books:

35mm handbook by Michael Langford, Viking O'Neill, 1988.

Exploring photography by Bryn Campbell, British Broadcasting Corp, 1978.

The travelling photographer's handbook by Julian Calder and John Garrett, Pan Books, 1985.

Photography, the art of seeing by Freeman Patterson, Van Norstrand Reinhold, 1979.

Contacts

Try to contact more experienced photographers willing to help you with your work. Local camera shops are a good place to start, and will often help solve any problems you may have. Find out if there's a camera club nearby.